www.kindermusik.com

ISBN 1-58987-044-1

Published in 2004 by Kindermusik International, Inc.

Printed in Mexico
First printing, February 2004

Zoo Train!

Lissa Rovetch
Illustrations by Brian Lies

Oh, we're riding on a train called the Allee-Allee O!
The Allee-Allee O! The Allee-Allee O!
Oh, we're riding on a train called the Allee-Allee O—
All through the zoo today!

Do you see the lions stretching in the sun,
Stretching in the sun, stretching in the sun?

And the happy, little penguins having so much fun,
So much fun in the zoo today!

Do you see the elephants? Their trunks swing
 and sway,
Trunks swing and sway, trunks swing and sway.

And the tall giraffes are munching leaves all day,
Munching leaves in the zoo today!

Do you see the kangaroos hopping up and down,
Hopping up and down, hopping up and down?

And the funny, fuzzy monkeys dancing all around,
All around the zoo today!

Do you see the polar bears playing in the snow,
Playing in the snow, playing in the snow?

And the silly, silver seals swimming high and low,
High and low in the zoo today!

Now we're going to the petting zoo with ponies, chicks,
and sheep,
Ponies, chicks, and sheep; ponies, chicks, and sheep!

And the tired baby animals say now it's time to sleep!
They'll sleep in the zoo today.

So back home we go on the Allee-Allee O,
The Allee-Allee O, the Allee-Allee O.
We say good-bye to the zoo and the Allee-Allee O.
We'll come back another day!

The Allee-Allee O
(song)

There's a big, long train called the Allee-Allee O,
The Allee-Allee O, the Allee-Allee O.
There's a big, long train called the Allee-Allee O,
Hooray for the zoo today!

To the zoo we go on the Allee-Allee O,
The Allee-Allee O, the Allee-Allee O.
To the zoo we go on the Allee-Allee O,
Hooray for the zoo today!

There are children marching on the Allee-Allee O,
The Allee-Allee O, the Allee-Allee O.
There are children marching on the Allee-Allee O,
Hooray for the zoo today!

There are children bouncing on the Allee-Allee O,
The Allee-Allee O, the Allee-Allee O.
There are children bouncing on the Allee-Allee O,
Hooray for the zoo today!

There are children gliding on the Allee-Allee O,
The Allee-Allee O, the Allee-Allee O.
There are children gliding on the Allee-Allee O,
Hooray for the zoo today!

There are children swaying on the Allee-Allee O,
The Allee-Allee O, the Allee-Allee O.
There are children swaying on the Allee-Allee O,
Hooray for the zoo today!

There are children hopping on the Allee-Allee O,
The Allee-Allee O, the Allee-Allee O.
There are children hopping on the Allee-Allee O,
Hooray for the zoo today!